Barry Chesney   Cathy Napier

ADDICTION:
One Day at a Time
with JESUS

Introduction

Families of the addicted get sick too. Many family therapists have written volumes on the codependency of family members who have a loved one riddled with addiction. The late John Bradshaw wrote numerous books exploring the damage done to families due to alcoholism and other addictions: drugs, gambling, sex, and even food (yes, there is such a thing as food addiction, also known as *disordered eating*). We think Bradshaw's best work was with his therapy and lectures on the inner child. He stated that a child can be influenced negatively by the dysfunctional dynamics of an alcohol- or drug-addicted home, which sometimes can be fueled by arguments and fighting. A wife or husband might hope for a relationship without a chemical in it. A parent who knows that their son or daughter is in the battle of a lifetime by being addicted to opioids has no relief from worry and anxiety. You may be able to identify with any of these scenarios or know someone else who does. You may wonder what God's word has to say about addictions, or if it has anything to say about them at all. Interestingly, yes, it does.

In 1 Corinthians 6, the apostle Paul explained that the human body of a follower of Jesus belongs to the Lord and is a temple of the Holy Spirit (v.19). Now, just stop and think about that for a moment. The human body has value in God's eyes. After all, Jesus had a human body and to this day has a glorified body in heaven at the right hand of the Father. There is nothing inherently sinful about the human body. Adam and Eve both had bodies before sin entered the world. Thus, we should care for our bodies and use them to glorify God.

The context of 1 Corinthians 6 highlights issues such as food and sexual immorality, two areas in which people experience addiction. In verse 12, Paul wrote, "'All things are lawful for me,' but not all things are helpful. 'All things are lawful for me,' but I will not be dominated by anything." The term "dominated" means someone has the right of control over someone or something else.[1] It is used in Luke 22:25 and refers to the benefactors who have authority over others. A common use of this term is to rulers' misuse of power.[2] Paul's point is that Christians enjoy freedom in life because Jesus has destroyed the one who has the power of death, namely the devil (Hebrews 2:14). Christians no longer must live with the fear of death because eternal life awaits them in heaven. But even though there is freedom from death in the Christian life, there is also the danger of being mastered by some things if Christians allow it. Christians can be addicted to substances, work, food, or sex if they allow it. Paul stated that he would not allow anything to win power over him; he would not give anything else, whether food or sexual immorality, authority

---

1. Frederick William Danker, ed., *A Greek-English Lexicon of the New Testament and other Early Christian Literature*, 3rd ed. (Chicago: The University of Chicago Press, 2000), 353.

2. Foerster, *Theological Dictionary of the New Testament*, ed. Gerhard Kittel, vol. 2 (Grand Rapids: Eerdmans, 1964), 574.

over him.[3] As Christians, we must live to serve King Jesus and not sin. Yes, we live in submission to our governing authorities (Romans 13:1), but no other substance or activity should exercise authority over us. We should not allow it.

People who are not Christians attempt to control their addiction by willpower. They do not have the resurrected power of Jesus inside of them to help them. And yet there are some Christians who battle addiction as well because they have given authority over their life to something else. Please read the story below and see if it resonates with you.

It's another sleepless night as I pick up my cell phone. The time is 2:40 a.m. and there's still no text from her. I've conditioned myself to listen intently for the notification ding. The only communication I would receive indicating she was alive was a text, never a phone call. My daily mantra whenever I received this text was, "She's drug free. She's alive." But when the texts stopped again, unfortunately, I knew she had relapsed—or worse, was dead. How many times have we reported her missing?

How many times have we stayed home instead of roaming the streets looking for her? We knew she was running with the wrong crowd. We knew that she was shooting up heroin. And we were in a state of terror most of the time. On this particular morning, I lay tossing and turning until 6:00 a.m. That seemed to be a good time to get out of bed. My body was tired, my eyes burning from lack of sleep. I was full of fear, sadness, and a deep sense of struggling to keep things together, especially my work.

She's twenty-four years old. I can't ground her or spank her. I

3. Ibid., 575.

can't put her in time-out or take her phone away. I can only hope and pray for her protection. I arrive at work, and that familiar wave of panic starts to well up inside me as another day moves on without a call or text. I cringe every time I get a call from an unknown number, fearing it will be the morgue. What's worse is my fear that she's having sex with strangers or being beaten up because she owes money to the wrong person. It hurts when your thoughts take you down a path that was unimaginable a few years ago. It hurts to think that if she were in prison, I could relax, because at least then I would know where she was every night.

This scene has been voiced to therapists in family sessions throughout the years, but unfortunately, this scenario plays out daily across America. Families from all over the United States—all over the world, for that matter—live in sheer panic for their loved ones. We're facing one of the worst health crises since the AIDS crisis, or the more recent Covid pandemic. Our children, our young adults, and even some elderly are dying in great numbers due to the opioid epidemic.

The chemically dependent will *not* wake up one day and decide they want to get help. They need their loved ones to intervene on their behalf. Otherwise, they will remain caught in the web of addiction and denial.

Let's think about this for a moment from a Christian worldview. The longest book in the Bible is Psalms. Many psalms were written by David, Israel's king for forty years. In 1 Samuel 13, the prophet Samuel spoke to King Saul and rebuked him for his unlawful sacrifice. Samuel said that God sought a man after His own heart who would replace Saul as King (v.14). That man was David. David was the youngest son of Jesse and was out taking care of sheep when Samuel came to anoint him as king (1 Samuel 16). Samuel anointed David and the Holy Spirit came upon him.

David did have a heart for God, but he was prone to sin, just like we are. In 2 Samuel 11, David committed sexual sin with Bathsheba, another man's wife. Then, David made matters worse by having her husband (Uriah) killed. This is one of the saddest and most tragic chapters in the Bible. Furthermore, David did not immediately confess his sin, as he should have. Instead, he took Bathsheba as his wife and had another child with her. While God allowed all of this to happen, He was not pleased with it. The end of 2 Samuel 11 says, "But the thing that David had done displeased the LORD" (v.27).

How would this sin pattern break in David's life? God raised the prophet Nathan to confront David. As described in 2 Samuel 7, God used the prophet Nathan to communicate a covenant God made with David that included his son Solomon and ultimately referred to the rule and reign of Jesus Christ. The prophet Nathan appeared again in 2 Samuel 12 when the Lord "sent Nathan to David" (v.1). Nathan did not instantly attack or confront David with his sin. However, Nathan told a story that captured David's attention. The essence of the story was this: a rich and a poor man both lived in the same city. The rich man had many flocks and herds, while the poor man had one little ewe lamb. This little lamb was well cared for by the poor man's family, and he considered the lamb like a daughter. One day a guest visited the rich man, who was unwilling to sacrifice one of his many lambs to feed the traveler. So, the rich man exerted his power and took the poor man's one daughter-like lamb, and had it killed so he could feed his guest.

Immediately, David saw the injustice done in this story and became angry. He said the rich man deserved to die for the wrong he had committed against the poor man! Nathan then said to David, *"You are the man!"* That is what David had done to Uriah, who was Bathsheba's husband.

David was already married, but it was not enough. He took another man's wife and then had Uriah killed. David was blind to his sin. So, God sent Nathan to communicate to David what He thought about David's sin. Even though David thought he committed his sin in secret, God knew what had happened. So how did David respond? Did he fly off in a rage against Nathan? Verse 13 says, "David said to Nathan, 'I have sinned against the LORD.'" In scripture, we read that God used the prophet, Nathan, to intervene in David's sinful life so that he could get right with God, experience forgiveness, and know the consequences that were to come as a result of his sin.

We should be thankful that the Lord sent Nathan to David because we have all benefited from it. "How so?" you might ask. David wrote Psalm 51 after Nathan confronted him with his sin. Psalm 51 offers hope during a struggle. For those overwhelmed and defeated by sin, the truth of Psalm 51 assures us that God can and will forgive us if we turn to Him in genuine repentance. In this psalm, David asked God to have mercy on him (v.1), for God to wash him from his iniquity and cleanse him from his sin (v.2), and for God to create in him a clean heart (v.10). He prayed God would restore to him the joy of His salvation (v.12). These are wonderful words to read and wonderful truths to experience. We have the privilege of reading and applying them to our lives because God sent Nathan to confront David, and he responded with repentance.

God can use us to intervene in the life of those battling addictions so the person will turn from the sin or substance they are addicted to and experience the freedom and forgiveness that God offers. You might think, "Yes, but I am not a prophet like Nathan." That may be true, but in Luke 10 we read that as followers of God, we must love God with all our heart, all our soul, all our strength, and all our mind. In addition, we must love our neighbor as ourselves (v.27). What does it mean to love our neighbor as ourselves? Thankfully, Jesus illustrated and explained that concept in verses 29–37. We know this story as the parable of the Good Samaritan. Loving one's neighbor means several things: we have compassion toward others (v.33), we give our time to help others (v.34), we endure personal inconvenience (v.34), we sacrifice personal finances (v.35), and we ensure the person is well taken care of (v.35). Loving one's neighbor can be messy, exhausting, and time-consuming. Yet by loving our neighbor, we reveal that we love God.

Notice in the parable of the Good Samaritan that the Samaritan did not stay long with the injured man. He sacrificed his time and resources, but he left the injured man in the care of the innkeeper. Presumably, the Samaritan had a life and responsibilities to assume, so he could not stay by the man's side for days on end. The Samaritan said he would repay the innkeeper if he spent more money when he returned (v.35). Intervening into an addict's life does not mean you spend every day for the rest of your life consumed with helping that person. It means you are faithful—you obey God and show God's love to that person when prompted by God. It is up to that person to receive the help offered. God may use you to intervene, and then you can go about your life while the injured person is under the watchful eye of a professional.

So, should we consider intervening in a loved one's life to help them break the cycle of addiction? We should. Doing so will be a way we show love to our neighbors.

As you consider an intervention into another's life, we want to equip you with tools for the process. Families don't need to feel helpless when they jump into action. Part one of this book is a guide to you, the family, to get out and become involved in the fight. This workbook will give families tools for self-help when they have an addicted loved one. This guide—a plan and manual of sorts—will enable you and your family to help loved ones in the throes of addiction.

We have entered four blank pages for your family to write down a plan that you will implement, so you can follow through with helping your family member get into wellness.

Chapter One

OPIOID: A substance used to treat moderate-to-severe pain. Highly addictive when used frequently.

The Centers for Disease Control and Prevention reported data for analysis on May 1, 2022. That data stated that there had been over 100,000 overdose deaths in the previous 12 months. Opioid abuse is the number one addiction among young people today, along with alcohol as the second chemical abused.

Opioid addiction often starts with someone having severe pain from an injury or surgery. A physician prescribes an opioid for pain management. The patient can become innocently addicted without even trying. Once they become addicted and can no longer get a legal prescription, they go outside the system or find a lenient physician to extend the prescription. Most of the time, an addict starts by buying pills off the street. Pills can lead to heroin (the latter is less expensive), either of which might be laced with fentanyl, which has been the culprit in the vast number of overdose deaths in our country. The pills and the heroin are coming from outside our country. Becoming addicted and seeking the drug by any means consumes the addict at a terrible cost to society, their family, and our healthcare system.

QUESTIONS

1. Do you have a family member who you're concerned may have an addiction to opioids? If so, describe the helplessness you feel as you watch them deteriorate.

_____

_____

_____

_____

_____

_____

_____

2. Describe how you have watched your loved one change physically and mentally.

_____

_____

_____

_____

_____

_____

_____

_____

_____

3. How are you taking care of yourself during this troubling time?

_____

_____

_____

_____

_____

_____

_____

_____

_____

_____

4. List the things you're doing that could be considered enabling.

_____

_____

_____

_____

_____

_____

_____

_____

_____

_____

5. What feelings are telling you that you're becoming codependent?

_____

_____

_____

_____

_____

_____

_____

_____

_____

_____

6. List the changes in you since you found out about the disease.

_____

_____

_____

_____

_____

_____

_____

_____

_____

_____

_____

7. List ways your relationship with your partner has changed.

_____

_____

_____

_____

_____

_____

_____

_____

_____

_____

8. How has your relationship with the Lord changed since you've had a loved one in the throes of addiction?

_____

_____

_____

_____

_____

_____

_____

_____

_____

_____

Chapter Two

ALCOHOLISM: The Centers for Disease Control and Prevention defines alcoholism as excessive binge drinking or consuming four or more drinks on an occasion for a woman, or five or more drinks on an occasion for a man. Heavy drinking is defined as 8 or more drinks per week for a woman or fifteen or more drinks per week for a man.

Consider the following story:

As the cold, damp wet awakens me, I'm puzzled as to what has happened. My clothes are drenched with sweat and the stench of vomit—a constant reminder of how sick this problem has made me. The smell of vomit hits my nostrils as if I had just walked across a landfill. The memory of the evening before is foggy. As much as I try to remember, I can't.

It's the early morning and I'm again awakened by the familiar taunting of the demon that's wearing on me. Slowly, I pull myself out of bed and go to the kitchen cabinet, where I keep the bottle of gin. I take a swig from the bottle and consider the insanity of the situation: the burning sensation is strangely enjoyable as it goes down my throat. The excitement comes as I tiptoe back to my room, realizing that, soon, I will get that much-needed sleep. I pause to remind myself that today I will need to go doctor shopping. I'm almost out of Percodan.

The morning brings the same life-numbing routine: get up and drink, go to work and drink, go to lunch and drink, come home and drink until bedtime. In my rational moments, I remember how it all started. But always the alcohol and pills keep recovery at a distance, as a mantra in my mind. I say over and over, "I need to quit . . ."

This is a true story of someone who knew they could not stop drinking. Maybe you've witnessed someone in your family exhibiting similar behavior. You may be thinking that your family member's alcohol abuse / addiction hasn't gotten that bad yet. But just wait—addiction of any kind has a progression.

As Christians, how can we lovingly help someone addicted to alcohol? Does the Bible have anything to say about alcohol consumption or abuse?[1] It absolutely does.[2] First, the Scriptures clearly prohibit the

---

1. For a very helpful article on wine as it appears in the Bible see Robert H. Stein, "Wine Drinking in New Testament Times," *Christianity Today*, June 20, 1975. Retrieved from https://www.christianitytoday.com/ct/1975/june-20/wine-drinking-in-new-testament-times.html on June 1, 2022. Stein argued there is a significant difference in the wine of New Testament times and the wine consumed today. Wine in New Testament times was heavily mixed with water compared to today's wine which has a much higher alcohol content.

2. The two most common words in the Old Testament that are used for alcohol are *shekar* (strong drink) and *yayin* (wine). These two words appear together as in Proverbs 20:1 above 21 times in the Old Testament. The word for strong drink refers to beer or any alcoholic beverage created from grain or fruit. The verbal

abuse of alcohol among Christians and especially spiritual leaders. In Ephesians 5:18, Paul wrote, "And do not get drunk with wine, for that is debauchery, but be filled with the Spirit." Proverbs 20:1 also presents alcohol abuse in a negative light by saying, "Wine is a mocker, strong drink a brawler, and whoever is led astray by it is not wise." (The NASB translation says, "And whoever is intoxicated by it is not wise.") In his qualifications for spiritual leadership in the church (elders and deacons) Paul said the elder must not be "a drunkard" (1 Tim. 3:3), a deacon must not be "addicted to much wine" (1 Tim. 3:8), and older women must not be "slaves to much wine" (Titus 2:3). There are many other Scriptures that also prohibit the abuse of alcohol.

Second, consider scriptural passages where wine was a neutral or part of celebratory events. In Genesis 14, Melchizedek brought out bread and wine to Abram (v.18). Job's children ate and drank wine

---

form of this word, *shakar*, which means to be drunk or intoxicated, is used nearly 60 times in the Old Testament and only 5 of the uses refer to something good or acceptable. The few times *shakar* refers to something good it does not normally refer to someone consuming alcohol. For example, in Genesis 43:34 Joseph's brothers were with Joseph in Egypt and they drank and became drunk with him. The point here is not that they drank to intoxication but they were reunited and enjoyed each other's friendly company. Strong drink was used in the drink offering as seen in Numbers 28:7 but this does not refer to personal intoxication since worship was the goal of the offering. Proverbs 31:6 says to give strong drink to the one who is perishing which presumably served a medicinal purpose offering temporary relief from pain. Taken from *Theological Wordbook of the Old Testament*, vol. 2., Harris, Archer, and Waltke, eds. (Chicago: Moody Press, 1980), 926-927. The term for wine (*yayin*) is used 140 times in the Old Testament for a drink at celebratory events and for use in offerings. Priests were forbidden to drink wine while ministering at the tent of meeting in Leviticus 10. Wine was a very intoxicating drink and probably contained about 7-10% alcohol content. Taken from *Theological Wordbook of the Old Testament*, vol. 1., Harris, Archer, and Waltke, eds. (Chicago: Moody Press, 1980), 865.

together (Job 1:13). In Nehemiah 2:1, Nehemiah was a cupbearer to the king and his job included tasting wine presented to the king. Psalm 104:14–15 describes God as the One who causes the grass to grow, so food and wine will spring from the earth to gladden the heart of man. At this point, the reader may be thinking, "Well, if God created wine and everything God created is good, then I can enjoy it whenever I want." That perspective should be tempered by our next point.

Third, Scripture limits the Christian's freedom in order to promote spiritual growth. In Romans 14, Paul wrote about causing other Christians to stumble spiritually. "Stumbling" refers to placing an object in someone else's path that causes them to misstep and experience a spiritual plateau or even decline. One stumbling block presented in Scripture is alcohol. Paul wrote, "It is good not to eat meat or drink wine or do anything that causes your brother to stumble" (v.21). Paul's point is to pursue the spiritual edification of another Christian and avoid anything that gets in the way of that—even alcohol. Avoiding the abuse of alcohol does not necessarily give Christians the right to drink, especially if near a younger brother or sister in the faith who might stumble because of it. Some Christians may choose to drink alcohol in private to prevent another from stumbling. Others may choose to abstain from alcohol altogether. They would not be the first. In the Old Testament era, a group called the Nazirites took a vow, which included abstaining from alcohol (Numbers 6:3–4). In the New Testament, John the Baptist, who foretold the ministry of Jesus, did not drink any wine (Luke 7:33).

While we cannot argue the Bible *prohibits* alcohol consumption for Christians, we can say it prevents abuse of alcohol. We should give careful thought to the question of whether Christians should drink at all. First, we should ask, does alcohol help me grow spiritually? If not, then is it wise to consume alcohol at all? Second, do I experience more of the joy of Jesus when I drink? Third, am I prone to overindulge? If so, it would be prudent to refrain from drinking alcohol—just as someone who was prone to overindulge in gambling would be wise to stay far from casinos. Finally, what story do I want told about myself one day at my funeral? Do I want alcohol to be part of that legacy? If not, then why spend time consuming alcohol in the present? These questions should help us think about the larger picture and help us determine a wise path forward on this issue.

PLEASE USE THESE BLANK PAGES for JOURNALING

_____
_____
_____
_____
_____
_____
_____
_____
_____
_____
_____
_____
_____
_____
_____
_____
_____
_____
_____
_____
_____
_____
_____
_____

_____
_____
_____
_____
_____
_____
_____
_____
_____
_____
_____
_____
_____
_____
_____
_____
_____
_____
_____
_____
_____
_____
_____
_____
_____
_____
_____
_____
_____

QUESTIONS

1. Do you have someone who you feel may have an alcohol problem? A family member, perhaps, or several? If you're free to list those who concern you, then please do below, so we may pray for them.

_____
_____
_____
_____
_____
_____
_____
_____
_____
_____

2. How has your loved ones' alcohol addiction affected you?

_____
_____
_____
_____
_____
_____
_____
_____
_____
_____

3. What changes have you seen in your family members' behavior?

_____

_____

_____

_____

_____

_____

_____

_____

_____

_____

4. Has your loved one had legal issues due to alcoholism? If yes, please explain.

_____

_____

_____

_____

_____

_____

_____

_____

_____

_____

5. Is your family member (or are your family members) in denial regarding the severity of their disease? If yes, please explain.

_____

_____

_____

_____

_____

_____

_____

_____

_____

_____

6. Do you see health issues your family member or members may have due to alcoholism? If so, please explain.

_____

_____

_____

_____

_____

_____

_____

_____

_____

_____

_____

7. Can you go back generations and trace the current alcoholism in your family?

_____

_____

_____

_____

_____

_____

_____

_____

_____

_____

_____

_____

Chapter Three

Understanding the Disease Concept of Alcoholism

The American Medical Association has declared that alcoholism is a disease. Alcoholism is a killer, but before it kills, it takes everything in its path—your family, your job, your money, your health, before finally killing you.

Henry R. Kranzler, MD, a professor of psychiatry in the Perlman School of Medicine at the University of Pennsylvania, is the first author of the study of the genetic drivers of heavy drinking and alcohol use disorder (AUD), the uncontrollable pattern of alcohol use commonly referred to as alcoholism. A team of researchers found 18 genetic variants of significance associated with either heavy alcohol consumption, AUD, or both. This study, one of many, is an example of why most alcoholics have difficulty stopping their addiction, and why the American Medical Association declared alcoholism a disease.

Robin Boom, who wrote *Sociological Aspects of the Disease Concept of Alcoholism*, stated on August 19, 1981, that the U.S. Postal Service issued a stamp carrying the message, "Alcoholism: You Can Beat It!" The stamp included a caduceus—a symbol associated with the National Council on Alcoholism. Drawing from publicity releases concerning the stamp, the *New York Times*' "Stamps" column for August 9 included, along with a thumbnail history of drinking and a favorable mention for the NCA, the following:

> Alcohol has been a pleasure to drink and a problem to mankind since the beginning of ancient civilization. Alcoholism is a disease—until recently a hidden and unrecognized disease. In the last several decades, there has been a growing recognition that alcoholism is a medical and not a moral problem, and a disease that can be treated effectively. There has been a marked change in the public attitude toward it . . .

Moral judgment has over the decades been a major factor in holding back alcoholism treatment. New approaches to alcoholism began after World War II, with the founding of Alcoholics Anonymous, and the research findings of the Yale School of Alcohol Studies. In 1951, the World Health Organization recognized alcoholism as a disease. The American Medical Association followed suit in 1956. The National Institute on Alcohol Abuse and Alcoholism was founded in 1971.

Gains have been made in the years since, although alcoholism still claims an estimated 10 million victims in the US each year. 30,000 deaths are attributed to cirrhosis of the liver alone. But alcohol misuse and alcoholism are also implicated in statistics on homicide, suicide, domestic violence, fire deaths, and drownings. Fifty percent of traffic fatalities are alcohol-related.

However, alcoholism is treatable, and alcoholics can and do recover.

This information is from Robin Room, The Alcohol Research Group, Institute of Epidemiology and Behavioral Medicine.

PLEASE USE THESE BLANK PAGES for JOURNALING

Chapter Four

The Protocol for Wellness for Your Addicted Loved One and Your Family

Intervention is something that comes between two other things or something that changes the course of something. An example of using intervention in drug and alcohol addiction would be a group of friends confronting a family member or friend about their drug use and asking the friend or family member to seek treatment. The intervention needs to come as a surprise to your loved one. Many good therapists do interventions. Be sure and check with a facility or private therapist and ask whom they would recommend for an intervention with the prospective patient and your family. Include friends, as well, who are willing to confront the behavior of your family member.

Schedule the intervention at a time when everyone who wishes to participate can be there. The interventionist will meet with everyone before the loved one arrives. Many families have staged an intervention under the auspices of having the loved one over for a scheduled dinner, and do not consider it deceit. Dinner can happen if everyone feels like it after the intervention.

Many times, a friend or other family member will need to help the loved one make the appointment. If left to their own devices, the addict is unlikely to arrive on time or even at all. The interventionist should get there an hour before the loved one is to show up. The interventionist will prep everyone on what and what *not* to say. It is important that there be no judging. Everything should be said with kindness and love. Remember, you're trying lovingly to get your loved one help.

Everyone attending the intervention will speak to the family member and give him or her an account of how they've seen their life deteriorate due to the family member's use of drugs. Please always stick with the *behavior* and do not shame the family member personally. If you know which drug they're using, name it. Be direct—but again, be kind.[1] Be specific about the marked difference in their behavior before using and after. Give concrete examples. Tell the person you love them and couldn't bear the thought of losing them. Tell them you want them to go for help now. Sometimes, an intervention can last several hours.

The interventionist will close the meeting, telling the family member that they have arranged for them to go for treatment. The interventionist will name the facility. The loved one will be encouraged to go right away. The end goal of an intervention is that the family member will go for treatment. The hope is that the entire family will participate in family therapy that is offered by most treatment facilities. We have seen some success when the entire family gets help through the facility and continues with family treatment long afterward.

A verse of scripture like the one below can bring peace to your soul

---

1. A great verse to apply here is Ephesians 4:15; "Rather, speaking the truth in love, we are to grow up in every way into him who is the head, into Christ." Truth must be spoken in love so that people grow spiritually and become more like Jesus Christ.

and comfort when you're going through difficult times with a loved one caught in the throes of addiction:

Psalm 91

He that dwelleth in the secret place of the most High shall abide under the shadow of the Almighty. I will say of the Lord, He is my refuge and my fortress my God; in Him will I trust. Surely he shall deliver thee from the snare of the fowler, from the noisome pestilence. He shall cover thee with his feathers, and under his wings shalt thou trust: his truth shall be thy shield and buckler. Thou shalt not be afraid for the terror by night; nor for the destruction that wasteth at noonday. A thousand shall fall at Thy side, and ten thousand at Thy right hand; but it shall not come nigh thee.

The wonderful above Psalm is meant to shine a light in your darkness. In verse 14, the Lord says, "Because he holds fast to me in love, I will deliver him; I will protect him because he knows my name." God's protection is predicated on a relationship with Him. As you are conducting an intervention, a great place to begin is the person's relationship with Jesus Christ. If the person has never received Jesus as Lord and Savior, start there. Share the gospel and encourage the person to receive Christ as Lord. If they receive Jesus, then they have access to God through Christ. Verse 15 says, "When he calls to me, I will answer him; I will be with him in trouble; I will rescue him and honor him." Almighty God offers His presence and rescue to the one who knows Him as Lord and Savior.

Imagine each line of Psalm 91 as soul food in times of trouble. You may want to pray each line as a request to God to put a protective shield around your loved one. I don't know anything more heartbreaking than watching a daughter or son going through the throes of alcohol / drug addiction. Families and loved ones get so desperate trying to fix the addiction that they become enablers. They become codependent, losing sight of their own needs—the addiction makes them sick too.

QUESTIONS

1. Do you feel that you're ready to plan an intervention for your family member? If yes, then who would you invite to participate?

_____

_____

_____

_____

_____

2. Write down things that you can do to help yourself during these difficult times.

_____

_____

_____

_____

_____

_____

_____

_____

_____

3. List those things you have let go of because of your involvement with a family member who has a problem with addiction. Examples: socializing, daily devotionals, etc.

_____

_____

_____

_____

_____

_____

_____

_____

_____

_____

4. Explain in detail how often your loved one is on your mind daily. Also, write the thoughts you have daily regarding your loved one's addiction.

_____

_____

_____

_____

_____

_____

_____

_____

_____

5. If you choose to do an intervention, then write down a list of changes you have seen in your family member. No shaming or critical statements—just statements that describe the changes in behavior. For example: "You used to love being involved in church, but you have fallen away." Or: "You used to play sports, but you have no interest anymore." Or: "You used to enjoy your book club, but you haven't attended in almost a year."

_____

_____

_____

_____

_____

_____

_____

_____

_____

_____

_____

_____

_____

_____

_____

_____

_____

6. Now it's time to list things you love about the person you knew before the addiction took hold of their life. Stay positive. Here's an example:

> The first is called, "What I love about you." I've heard many positive things spoken in exercises to the family member. I've watched the face of the family member receiving the message. The face tells the story—whether it's a slight smile or a huge, beaming smile. Afterward, I would ask the client, "What was the best part of the family work?" Invariably, I'd hear, "I had no idea that my mom thinks I'm kind. I had no idea that my dad thinks I'm strong." Sadly, this may have been the only time the patient had heard this positive feedback.

I want to remind the reader of the wisdom of Psalm 32:

> As long as I kept silent,
> My bones wasted away:
> I groaned all day.

These lines say it all too well for the family therapy program and family therapy sessions. We can't keep silent—we must talk about it.

_____

_____

_____

_____

_____

(continued on next page)

_____
_____
_____
_____
_____
_____
_____
_____
_____
_____
_____
_____
_____
_____
_____
_____

Your preparation for doing an intervention
is complete. Now you will need to find an
interventionist and set the date.

PLEASE USE THESE BLANK PAGES for JOURNALING

Addiction keeps both the chemically dependent family member and their family in bondage. They are only free when the substance is removed from the family unit. When the family member is in recovery, the blessings that both the family unit and their loved one in recovery will experience are:

1. To be aware of and embrace our place in God's universe.
2. To recognize ourselves as children of the one true God.
3. To experience the joys and suffering in life with feelings.
4. To be honest and have caring relationships with people who cross our path.
5. To be able to laugh and to see the humor in our relationship with addicted loved ones.
6. To be used by God to plant the seeds of hope in a recovery that will touch others' lives.
7. To grow old gracefully and with great courage.

Chapter Five

God created sex and designed it for one man and one woman to enjoy and procreate within the context of marriage. Remember that it was God who created Eve when Adam was asleep and brought her to him.[1] After this, the end of Genesis 2 says that Adam and Eve were naked and were not ashamed.[2] So what happened? Why is it that sex for so many today brings shame and guilt instead of joy and pleasure, as God intended? The short answer is sin. After Adam and Eve sinned against God in Genesis 3:6,[3] the very next verse says their eyes were opened and they knew they were naked. There was no problem with

---

1. Genesis 2:22 says, "And the rib that the LORD God had taken from the man he made into a woman and brought her to the man."

2. In his book entitled *God on Sex*, Danny Akin wrote, "Sex is good; it is God's gift. It should be enjoyed and enjoyed often. This good gift of God will find its fullest expression realized when a man and woman give themselves completely to each other in the marriage relationship" (3).

3. "So when the woman saw that the tree was good for food, and that it was a delight to the eyes, and that the tree was to be desired to make one wise, she took of its fruit and ate, and she also gave some to her husband who was with her, and he ate."

being naked before the couple sinned. But now the couple tried to hide their nakedness by sewing fig leaves into loincloths, and they tried to hide from the presence of God.[4]

Sin leads to hiding; hiding what we have done for fear of being found out. In the context of sexual addiction, hiding our sin can manifest as the frequent erasing of pornographic websites on our internet history, or hiding purchases of pornographic magazines or prostitutes to feed our sexual addiction. Sin may bring temporary pleasure, but it is guaranteed to bring shame and a strategy to hide the sin. It is interesting that the rest of the Biblical story after Genesis 3 explains that humans are blind to their spiritual condition and need God to open their eyes so they can be born again through faith in Jesus.[5] This means the answer to any addiction is a relationship with God through His Son, Jesus. Only God has the power to break the chains of addiction in our lives.

Sexual addiction is the most difficult type of addiction to stop due to the biological aspects of the sex drive. The sex drive is as strong as the craving for food and water. Sexual addiction has a progression that ultimately leads to devastation. The good news is that it is possible to intervene early enough to keep it from progressing to the point where it takes everything. Young men and women in their teens are curious about sex, especially during puberty. The internet has taken advantage of this curiosity and given teens easy access to pornography. Parents can and should intervene in their lives earlier

---

4. Genesis 3:8 says, "And they heard the sound of the LORD God walking in the garden in the cool of the day, and the man and his wife hid themselves from the presence of the LORD God among the trees of the garden."

5. Andrew Steinmann, *Genesis*, vol. 1 (Downers Grove: 2019), 69.

so that the addiction doesn't take hold and give them an unhealthy view of God's gift of sexuality, which was designed to be used in the confines of marriage.[6]

Followers of Jesus are certainly not immune from parenting children who struggle with sexual addiction. Consider Eli, the priest in the days of Samuel. 1 Samuel 2:12 introduces us to Eli's sons, saying they "were worthless men. They did not know the LORD." Eli heard all that his sons were doing to all of Israel, and their sexual immorality when they were serving at the entrance of the temple. The very place where God should have been honored—namely the "tent of meeting"—was where sexual immorality transpired. Eli confronted his sons and told them of the bad report he had heard (1 Sam. 2:24). But Eli's sons would not listen to their father (v.25). We believe there are two reasons for this. First, Eli's sons did not know the Lord. They did not worship God nor have any inner conviction that their sin was wrong. If we do not honor God as the primary authority in our lives, then we will find it challenging to submit to any other authority. Second, Eli was old (verse 22 says that Eli was very old). He waited too long before confronting his boys with their sins. Parents must know what their children are viewing on their electronic devices. It takes hard work, time, and energy to do this, but it is essential for shepherding the hearts of children.

---

6. One practical way of parents shepherding their children through the teenage years is for dads to read through a book together with their son or moms read a book together with their daughters and discuss. Books have a way of surfacing issues and promoting discussion that might not otherwise occur. Two book suggestions are *Every Man's Battle: Winning the War on Sexual Temptation One Victory at a Time* by Stephen Arterburn and Fred Stoeker; the female version is *Every Woman's Battle* by Shannon Ethridge and Stephen Arterburn. A second recommended book is *Unwanted: How Sexual Brokenness Reveals Our Way to Healing* by Jay Stringer.

If parents do not shepherd their children in their sexuality, then they are abdicating their responsibility and giving an opportunity to the secular culture in which we live, which is hostile toward Biblical Christianity. Research done with 3800 men and women who struggled with unwanted sexual behavior revealed that half of them had mothers who did not speak with them about sex at all. Almost two thirds of them had fathers who did not speak with them about sex.[7] Only 8% had a healthy conversation about sex with their mother, and only 5% had a helpful conversation about sex with their father.[8]

But teenagers are not the only ones battling sexual addiction. In fact, as we will see in the pages ahead, many adults in the Bible engaged in sexual sin. We will look at a few examples and see the consequences these people had to endure but also the hope that arose because of faith in God. God's word does not gloss over real-life struggles. For that, we are thankful, because we can learn from their failures and examples. Every human except Jesus, the God-man, has a sinful nature, and we are all prone to sexual temptation.

Adult men and women today experience an increase in internet connections aimed at "hooking up." Marriages are destroyed by this type of sexual addiction. God's word is clear on His plan for sexuality; "For this is the will of God, your sanctification: that you abstain from sexual immorality; that each of you knows how to control his own body in holiness and honor, not in the passion of lust like the Gentiles who

---

7. Jay Stringer, *Unwanted: How Sexual Brokenness Reveals Our Way to Healing* (Carol Stream, IL: Tyndale House, 2018), 39.

8. Ibid.

do not know God."[9] The Greek term for sexual immorality. Believers in Jesus, whether married or unmarried, must stay away from any form of sexual immorality.[10] In the big picture, God is making His people into the image of Jesus Christ, and sexual immorality interferes with that process.[11] Jesus is holy and without sin, and that is why God's people should be growing in holiness as well. The Christian's body is a temple of the Holy Spirit (see 1 Corinthians 6:19), and no person's body is their own. We belong to Jesus and must live for His will. Our bodies must be set apart for God's purposes, not in passionate lust after our own desires.

Human tendency is to base our morality and our views concerning sexuality on the culture in which we live. That is a dangerous approach, especially when we witness a moral revolution that includes cohabitation among couples who have yet to marry. A Pew Research Center Study revealed that 69% of Americans said that cohabitation is acceptable even if a couple does not plan to marry.[12] These demonstrate the reality that Christians must base their morality on God's revealed will in the Bible rather than the culture's moral

---

9. 1 Thessalonians 4:3-4.

10. Hauck / Schulz, *Theological Dictionary of the New Testament*, vol. 4, Gerhard Friedrich, ed., (Grand Rapids: Eerdmans, 1968), 595.

11. Romans 8:29 says, "For those whom he foreknew he also predestined to be conformed to the image of his Son, in order that he might be the firstborn among many brothers."

12. https://www.pewresearch.org/fact-tank/2019/11/06/key-findings-on-marriage-and-cohabitation-in-the-u-s/. Accessed on August 8, 2022.

agenda.[13] Hebrews 13:4 says, "Let marriage be held in honor among all, and let the marriage bed be undefiled, for God will judge the sexually immoral and adulterous." The first word in a Greek sentence normally indicates that word's importance, and the first term in verse 4 is "honor." That is how Christians should treat marriage; we must honor the institution that God has established. How do we do that?

We honor God in marriage when we guard the marital relationship by exercising faithfulness to God and each other. The word for "undefiled" means "pure" and indicates a dual focus of purity in one's relationship with God and sexual purity within the marriage.[14] The marriage bed is defiled through extramarital affairs that break trust and inflict serious harm upon the spouse[15] Although an affair may go undetected by that spouse, God sees it, knows about it, and will hold the guilty party accountable. The end of verse 4 says that God will judge the sexually immoral and adulterous. While the culture may approve of sexual immorality, God is against it, and He will issue the final verdict. In the larger context of the book of Hebrews, the

---

13. Danny Akin wrote, "God knows nothing of casual sex, because in reality there is no such thing. What is often called casual sex is always costly. Sexually transmitted diseases (STDs), unexpected pregnancy, and psychological and spiritual scars are some of the results, and the price paid, because we have approached God's good gift of sex all too casually. Sexual attraction is inevitable. It is what God intended. However, unless we follow God's plan, we will miss out on His best and suffer the painful and tragic consequences in the process." See Daniel Akin, *God on Sex: The Creator's Ideas About Love, Intimacy and Marriage* (Nashville: Broadman & Holman, 2003), 3.

14. Frederick William Danker, *A Greek-English Lexicon of the New Testament and other Early Christian Literature*, 3rd ed., (Chicago: University of Chicago, 2000), 54.

15. Thomas R. Schreiner, *Hebrews* (Nashville: B&H Publishing, 2015), 413.

author's argument is that one way to fall away from the faith is to give oneself over to sexual sin.[16]

Sexual sin appears enticing on the surface. It appeals to our sinful, fleshly desires, and our longing to satisfy that urge. The former King of Israel, Solomon, knew too well about sexual desire. He had 700 wives and 300 concubines who negatively impacted his spiritual life.[17] In Proverbs 5, Solomon wrote to his son, instructing him to stay far away from the "strange" or "forbidden" woman. The forbidden woman is the adulteress—the woman who is not his son's wife. She possessed seductive speech—as Solomon put it, her lips dripped honey and her speech was smoother than oil (verse 3). There is an intrinsic and inseparable connection between speech and sex.[18] Adulterous affairs are rarely based solely on physical attraction. Often there has been affirmation communicated from the woman to the man, and there has been a willing listener and encouraging man who has caught the attention of that woman. Affairs often arise because the guilty party discovers another person who meets an unmet need in his or her life. When that need—whether it is for kind words, a listening ear, or empathy—is met, attraction is born, and an affair is a likely result. In Proverbs 5, it is the woman who entices the man with speech. But in our day, it could just as easily be the man who seduces the woman through romantic poems, love songs, and empty promises.

---

16. Ibid.

17. See 1 Kings 11:3; "He had 700 wives, who were princesses, and 300 concubines. And his wives turned away his heart."

18. Bruce K. Waltke, *The Book of Proverbs*, vol. 1 (Grand Rapids: Eerdmans, 2004), 308.

The forbidden woman's speech appears irresistible and advertises fulfillment. But in the end, as verse 4 explains, she is bitter as wormwood and sharp as a two-edged sword. Verse 4 says "in the end," which refers to what happens after the extra-marital affair occurs. The allure of sin does not last forever; at some point reality sets in and consequences appear. After the fleeting pleasure of sin, the man realizes this woman's speech was only a show; she appeared to drip honey but the speech carried a sting with it.[19] Wormwood is often connected to the word "gall" which is a bitter and poisonous plant.[20] The man has inflicted harm upon himself because of his sexual misconduct, and he no longer experiences lips that are smoother than oil; instead, her words are cutting like a double-edged sword. Solomon warned his son against the foolishness of sexual misconduct in marriage, and in the last part of Proverbs 5 (verses 15-23) exhorted him to enjoy sexual intimacy with his own wife.

In addition to the connection between speech and sex, there is also a link between sight and sex, especially for males. In Proverbs 6, Solomon referred to the adulteress's beauty and her eyelashes; "do not let her capture you with her eyelashes" (verse 25b). Right before this, he said, "Do not desire her beauty in your heart" (verse 25a). The Hebrew term for desire here means "to lust" and is used in the Ten Commandments in reference to coveting.[21] According to Jesus, if a man looks at a woman with lustful intent he has already committed

---

19. Ibid., 309.

20. Ibid.

21. Allen P. Ross, *The Expositor's Bible Commentary*, Frank Gaebelein, ed., vol. 5 (Grand Rapids: Zondervan, 1991), 937.

adultery with her in his heart.[22] Solomon told his son not to lust after an adulteress in his heart and to not be seduced by her painted eyes and flirtatious looks.[23] In Proverbs 6:26 Solomon gave the explanation for his instruction; "for the price of a prostitute is only a loaf of bread, but a married woman hunts down a precious life." The price of paying a prostitute may not appear high in the beginning, but according to Solomon, adultery will cost the man his very life.[24] It may cost him his marriage and children or even his career. Sexual sin carries serious consequences.

We must see sexual sin—whether it is lust in the heart of the act of sexual immorality—for what it is: sin against God. One man in the Old Testament certainly knew this—Joseph. Joseph was a godly man who endured mistreatment from his brothers yet maintained a heavenly perspective. Joseph's brothers sold him into slavery and the Ishmaelites took him to Egypt.[25] Even in Joseph's mistreatment, God was with him and gave hm a favor. Joseph became a successful man[26] and worked for an Egyptian master named Potiphar as overseer of his house. Joseph was handsome, and Potiphar's wife took notice, saying

---

22. Matthew 5:28.

23. Ibid.

24. Ibid.

25. See Genesis 37:28.

26. See Genesis 39:2.

to him, "Lie with me."[27] Yet, in the heat of the moment of sexual temptation, Joseph had the perspective to think objectively about his life and about how sexual sin would displease God. He realized that Potiphar trusted him, placing all his estates in his care. The only thing that Potiphar had withheld from Joseph was his wife.

Joseph determined that she was off-limits because she was married.[28] He concluded, "How then can I do this great wickedness and sin against God?" If Joseph chose to have an affair with Potiphar's wife, perhaps Potiphar would have never discovered it. Nonetheless, it would have been a sin against God. The crime would not be against Potiphar alone; it was an offense against God.[29] Sexual sin is great wickedness. According to the Mosaic Law in Deuteronomy 22:22, if a man is found in a sexual relationship with another man's wife, both should die. Moses concluded, "So you shall purge the evil from Israel." Joseph demonstrated faithfulness to God, whereas earlier in Genesis, Adam and Eve did not when they ate fruit from the forbidden tree.[30] Joseph understood what was forbidden—namely, Potiphar's wife— and realized the consequences of such an evil action.

Potiphar's wife did not take "no" for an answer and continued approaching Joseph for a sexual encounter. Genesis 39:10 says that she spoke to Joseph day after day, but he would not listen to her or lie beside her or be with her. Joseph had enough wisdom to stay away

27. Genesis 39:7.

28. Genesis 39:9.

29. Kenneth A. Mathews, *Genesis*, vol. 2., Nashville: B&H Publishers, 2005, 734.

30. See Genesis 3:6.

from Potiphar's wife. Success in abstaining from sexual sin, at least in part, rests on avoiding situations that lead to it. Pastor Tommy Nelson once said that couples who are dating should not allow themselves to get in the back seat of a car and say they were suddenly "tempted." Couples who are dating and not yet married must have boundaries in place to prevent situations that will arouse sexual desires and foster sexual temptation.

One day, Joseph went to work in Potiphar's house. It was empty except for Potiphar's wife. She took full advantage of the situation and became more aggressive with her proposal. She grabbed his garment this time and said, "Lie with me."[31] We are not told that Joseph even said a word. The rest of Genesis 39:12 says that "he left his garment in her hand and fled and got out of the house." He immediately removed himself from the situation. Paul wrote something similar to the church at Corinth, a city known for sexual immorality: "Flee from sexual immorality. Every other sin a person commits is outside the body, but the sexually immoral person sins against his own body." Christians cannot flirt with sexual temptation. We must avoid it at all costs and if we are approached with a sexual proposal, we must immediately leave the situation.

What happens when someone does not flee from sexual temptation? The Bible gives us an example of that scenario as well in the story of Samson. Samson certainly knew something about sexual addiction. Samson led Israel as a judge for twenty years. The angel of the Lord appeared to Samson's mother prior to his birth and said she would have a son; the child would be a Nazirite from the womb.[32] The Nazirite

---

31. Genesis 39:12.

32. See Judges 13:3-5.

Vow is explained in Numbers 6. In short, it was a vow of separation from certain things, like cutting one's hair with a razor, or touching a dead body. It also required abstaining from wine and strong drinks in order to give one's self completely to God. But Samson did not live his life with complete devotion to God. In fact, he did not even marry an Israelite woman. Samson married a Philistine woman in Judges 14, but that did not end well since in his hot anger he left his wife and went back to his parents' house.

Meanwhile, Samson's father-in-law gave Samson's wife to another man.[33] In the very next chapter, we see Samson engaged in a sexual relationship with a prostitute.[34] Before long, that relationship was no longer enough for Samson. Verse 4 says that "after this, he loved a woman in the Valley of Sorek, whose name was Delilah." The Philistine leaders paid her to seduce Samson, and she was eventually successful. Samson's love for foreign women—women outside of Israel who did not have his best interests at heart—cost him dearly. He shared his heart with Delilah, meaning he told her the source of his strength, which was that a razor had never been used on his head.[35] Sadly, this is often the source of sexual sin; men and women are looking for people to share their hearts with. They want someone to understand them, and so they fantasize through pornography, or they find another willing partner to engage in sin with.

---

33. See Judges 15:2.

34. See Judges 16:1.

35. See Judges 16:17.

Sharing his heart with a foreign woman cost Samson dearly.[36] The Philistine leaders seized him and gouged out his eyes. It is tragic that probably the last thing Samson saw was the woman he loved, who obviously did not love him in return, but instead manipulated him and turned him over to her leaders. Sexual sin brings devastating consequences. The act or relationship we put our hope in will always disappoint us.

The good news here is that God was not yet finished with Samson. If you are reading this amid sexual addiction, God is not finished with you either. After Samson's eyes were gouged out, Judges 16:22 says the hair on his head began to grow again. Perhaps Samson recommitted himself to God after suffering blindness and experiencing the emptiness of sin. The growth of hair offered hope that Samson could still play a role in God's plan for Israel.[37] Indeed, God still had a plan to use Samson. A group of Philistines gathered, and Samson was called upon to entertain them. While there, Samson prayed to God. We do not know how long it had been since Samson prayed. Nonetheless, Samson called to the Lord and said, "O Lord God, please remember me and please strengthen me only this once, O God, that I may be avenged on the Philistines for my two eyes."[38] Then Samson

---

36. God loves all people but He instructed Israelite males to avoid marrying non-Israelite women because they would turn the Israelites hearts away from God and toward their false gods. God's prohibition was based on the unbelief of the non-Israelite women rather than race. See 1 Kings 11:2.

37. Daniel I. Block, *Judges, Ruth* (Nashville: B&H Publishers, 1999), 463.

38. Judges 16:28.

requested to die with the Philistines.[39]

God heard Samson's prayer and gave Samson strength one more time. Samson pushed on the pillars and the house fell, killing everyone in it, including Samson.[40] Samson's primary request to God was "Please remember me." The term "remember" here means to take note of, to act on behalf of.[41] Samson wanted to participate in God's plan, and God responded positively. God in His mercy decided to intervene on Samson's behalf and answer his plea.

What does Samson's story teach us about sexual addiction? For those who are shackled by the chains of sexual addiction, hope and freedom are found in God. Only God can break the chains of sexual addiction in our lives. His power is available for any person who calls upon Him. Samson knew about God but failed to live his life for God. Yet, when he finally called upon God, God responded with mercy and deliverance. In Samson's final prayer, he used three different names of God—Adonai, Yahweh, and Elohim—which indicates he knew God personally and he knew where to turn in need.[42] Maybe some of you reading this have personally engaged in sexual sin or you know someone else who has. Overwhelmed by the shame and guilt, you sense that God is finished with you. Maybe it has been a while since

---

39. See Judges 16:30.

40. See Judges 16:30. Samson killed more at his death than he had killed when he lived.

41. Block, *Judges, Ruth*, 467.

42. Arthur E. Cundall, Leon Morris, *Judges & Ruth* (Downers Grove, IL: Inter-Varsity Press, 1968), 180-81.

you prayed to God. Perhaps you even think to yourself, "How could God ever use me again after what I have done?" But take heart from Samson's story—if we turn to God in genuine repentance, God will hear, and He will have mercy on us.

David experienced God's mercy and forgiveness after falling into sin. David committed sexual sin with another man's wife in 2 Samuel 11. David took the initiative and inquired about a woman he saw bathing. Her name was Bathsheba and had her brought to his home.[43] Through this sexual encounter, the woman became pregnant. Next, David strategized to hide his sin. He eventually had Bathsheba's husband, Uriah, killed, even though he was an honorable and loyal man who fought in Israel's army. After Uriah's death and the period of mourning that ensued, David sent for Bathsheba and she became his wife. In reading 2 Samuel 11 it appears that David got away with the sexual sin and the murder of Uriah unscathed—until we read the last part of the final verse in the chapter; "But the thing that David had done displeased the LORD." God knew exactly what had transpired and He did not approve.

As David's example demonstrates, sexual addiction destroys families. When a family member—whether a husband, a wife, a boy, or a girl—starts down the road of viewing pornography or having an affair, the family unit starts to crack. If there isn't some type of intervention, the affair progresses. Intervention can be within the family unit at first. If the sexual acting out hasn't stopped at that point, a therapist can help.

The financial damages can be sizeable when the disease of sexual addiction starts to escalate. Pornography isn't as satisfying as it once was, so looking for a sexual partner becomes paramount. Men and

---

43. 2 Samuel 11:4.

women will look within their scope of business for a willing partner. For men, the escalation will go beyond just an affair. Men tend to look for call girls or prostitutes when the addiction has progressed. The "mind twist" is the idea that anonymous sex without restraint will become the norm instead of something unusual.

Credit cards are charged to the maximum by pulling out cash withdrawals so the sex addict can pay for call girls or prostitutes. Some pornographic internet sites are costly as well.

Many sex addicts will tell you that when the addiction escalates, they can no longer perform their jobs due to the mental interference of daily planning their next sexual encounter. The addict will find excuses to leave work early or to avoid work altogether.

Sex addicts are prone to depression because of the feeling of not being able to stop, or the fear that their families will find out about their secret life. Often the behavior "outs" the addict, and they are left with anxiety and fear that they're going to lose their family as a result. The sex addict often only seeks treatment when the family finds out, or when there are other consequences.

David endured substantial consequences because of his sin. First, the child that resulted from the sexual sin died. The Lord afflicted the child, and he became sick.[44] David fasted, wept, and prayed to God on behalf of the child, yet the child did not recover. Second, David experienced turmoil within his own family. David's son, Absalom, was infatuated with his sister Tamar, and took advantage of her by forcing himself upon her. The Scripture says that "he violated her and lay with her."[45] When David heard about it, he was very angry, but

---

44. 2 Samuel 12:15.

45. 2 Samuel 13:14.

what could he do?[46] He had lost his moral authority with his children because of his own sin. Sin robs us of influence with our own family and friends. Who wanted to listen to David give a lecture on moral purity after his own personal failure?

Next, David experienced political upheaval when his son Absalom tried to steal the throne of Israel from him. Absalom rose early in the morning and went to the gate of the city. He caused people to doubt David's leadership. He asserted himself, saying how he would lead if he were in charge. The Bible says that "Absalom stole the hearts of the men of Israel."[47]

The next scene in David's story is so sad. He had to leave his home in Jerusalem because Absalom had stirred up a national rebellion against his dad. After David was gone, Absalom had sexual relations with David's concubines. The family upheaval that David experienced in his life can be traced back to his sexual sin. God clearly told David this through the prophet Nathan; "Behold, I will raise up evil against you out of your own house. And I will take your wives before your eyes and give them to your neighbor, and he shall lie with your wives in the sight of this sun. For you did it secretly, but I will do this thing before all Israel and before the sun."[48]

God's word came true. In plain sight, for all of Israel to view, Absalom had sexual relations with his father's concubines.[49]

---

46. See 2 Samuel 13:21.

47. 2 Samuel 15:6b.

48. 2 Samuel 12:11-12.

49. 2 Samuel 16:22.

The final stage of sexual addiction is when the addict's mind, life, and soul are in bondage. Sin promises pleasure, but it only produces pain. If there's anger mixed with sex, or if there are no boundaries, then legal issues become involved in the form of abuse or rape. Unless there is some type of intervention to halt the sex addict's path to destruction, they end up with all the consequences of this disease, which are as follows:

1. Families are destroyed due to the marriage bed being interrupted. Sex with a husband or wife is no longer exciting, but mundane and boring. Sexual immorality with a total stranger becomes more exciting.

2. Financial problems escalate due to running up credit cards. The addict spends money on pornographic material or prostitutes. An enormous amount of money is spent in topless bars. The "mind twist" is this: men throw money at women who are performing in topless bars, thinking the women are in love with them. The performers are merely performing—flirting with the men so the men pay more for their attention. Visiting topless bars becomes an addiction in itself—due to the attention the men feel is genuine but is just a delusion.

3. Job losses due to the addict never having any relief from planning and reviewing their sexual escapades, leaving work early, or skipping work to hire prostitutes or call girls.

4. Depression sets in due to the addict thinking that nothing in their world is exciting anymore. Everything around them seems too normal and boring. Several factors contribute to

the lack of enjoyment of normal things. First, is the increase in the brain chemical dopamine, which goes into overdrive during an addiction. Dopamine does not respond to a normal routine, and so the addict must get their hit some other way. Second, depression creeps in slowly as life starts to crumble, with the loss of a job, relationships, money, etc.

5. Sexually transmitted diseases (STDs) due to sexual activity with escorts, prostitutes, or strangers met on the internet. Many men and women have unknowingly carried an STD home to their partners.

6. Daily, the addict lives with extreme stress and anxiety. The escalation of the disease occupies their mind every nanosecond of the day. The wreckage is no longer a secret— everything that's happening points to the sexual addiction.

7. For the Christian, a veil of darkness has now replaced the once-cherished peace. Christians will long for what they once had, with no path to get back there except to ask Jesus for forgiveness and work to get into recovery. They will wake up in spiritual darkness and go to bed in spiritual darkness again, not to be confused with depression. The sweet intimate relationship they had with Jesus is now replaced by something sinister that has set out to destroy them and all associated with them.

8. Those in the throes of sexual addiction also commonly partake of drugs and alcohol. So, the sex addict often has additional nightmares in their life. Cocaine gives the sex

addict a false sense of reality. They assume that cocaine enhances the sex act, only to realize that it is just another expensive addiction.

The consequences of our sin can be devastating, but there is hope. How so? Think of the good that came from David's struggles. From this example, we first see the need to confess our sins to God. After a period, Nathan confronted David[50] concerning his sin, and David admitted that he had sinned against the Lord.[51] At this point, David wrote Psalm 51. This psalm is about confession of sin and repentance. David pleaded to God for mercy and confessed his wrongdoing. That must be the first step that we take after sexual sin. God is merciful and will forgive, but we must genuinely admit our sin to Him. One of the great statements in this psalm is verse 10—"Create in me a clean heart, O God, and renew a right spirit within me." Confession of sin to God will lead to a clean heart and a right spirit.

Second, we see the forgiveness of God on display. Most likely, Psalm 32 was written following David's sexual sin and his murder of Uriah.[52] David detailed the misery that men and women experience when we refuse to confess our sins to God. Verse 4 says that day and night God's hand was heavy upon him, and his strength was dried up as in the heat of summer. We all know what it is like to experience utter exhaustion after working in the yard in the sweltering heat, or after

---

50. See 2 Samuel 12.

51. See 2 Samuel 12:13.

52. Thomas L. Constable, "Psalms." https://www.planobiblechapel.org/tcon/notes/html/ot/psalms/psalms.htm. Accessed on August 18, 2022.

standing in the hot sun for an extended period. It is draining. That is David's metaphor for the toll that sin takes upon us. The solution is to admit our sin to God, and that is what David did. He wrote, "I acknowledged my sin to you, and I did not cover my iniquity" (verse 5a). Then, notice what happened; God "forgave the iniquity of my sin." If we confess our sins, God will forgive them. No lecture. No guilt trip. Only God's forgiveness.

Third, we learn from David's mistakes that God can protect us moving forward. God is forgiving and He can restore the years the locusts have taken away.[53] As David fled Jerusalem from Absalom, he wrote Psalm 3. In this psalm, David affirmed his trust in God. Verse three is a powerful declaration of David's faith in God, "But you, O LORD, are a shield about me, my glory, and the lifter of my head." The consequences of David's sin were real but so was God's protection. God lifted David's head above the storm around him so that he could experience the presence and protection of God during his difficulties. If you are enduring the painful consequences of your sin, pause right now and from the depths of your heart quote verse three to God. David was talking to God in prayer. You can too. And you too can enjoy the presence of God and His peace and protection amid your struggle.

If you or someone you know is experiencing sexual addiction, consider using negative / positive imaging to help. The mantra used daily with prayer is: "Jesus I don't want anything to grieve the Holy Spirit. I know my sexual addiction is keeping me from a closer walk with you. Jesus, I want my daily walk with you, not my addiction."

Billy Graham said, "Only when we understand the holiness of God will we understand the depth of our sin."

---

53. See Joel 2:25.

PLEASE USE THESE BLANK PAGES for JOURNALING

THERAPY for the SEX ADDICT

NEGATIVE / POSITIVE IMAGING

1. Write down your personal goals.

_____

_____

_____

_____

_____

_____

_____

_____

_____

_____

_____

_____

2. Write down your relationship goals.

_____

_____

_____

_____

_____

_____

_____

_____

_____

_____

_____

3. Write down the kind of relationship you want with the Lord—
   be specific.

   _____

   _____

   _____

   _____

   _____

   _____

   _____

   _____

   _____

   _____

4. What is your purpose in life? This can be several things. List as
   many as you can and be specific.

   _____

   _____

   _____

   _____

   _____

   _____

   _____

   _____

   _____

   _____

5. Write down your need to overcome sexual addiction.

_____
_____
_____
_____
_____
_____
_____
_____
_____
_____
_____
_____

6. What kind of legacy do you want to leave behind after your death?

_____
_____
_____
_____
_____
_____
_____
_____
_____
_____
_____

7. After answering the questions, write down positive images in your mind. For example, imagine yourself taking up some type of exercise program. Imagine yourself doing that exercise and think of the satisfaction it would bring you. Be creative and think outside the box. Remember that sexual addiction took everything positive in your life.

_____

_____

_____

_____

_____

_____

_____

_____

_____

_____

_____

_____

_____

_____

_____

_____

_____

_____

8. Now, create a negative image based on the questions above. For example, seeing your family being destroyed by your addiction, or a child following in your footsteps after watching your behavior.

_____
_____
_____
_____
_____
_____
_____
_____
_____
_____

9. Write down the cues/triggers that contribute to your sexual addiction.

_____
_____
_____
_____
_____
_____
_____
_____
_____
_____
_____
_____

PLEASE USE THESE BLANK PAGES for JOURNALING

The Sex Addicts' Protocol for Wellness:

The good news is that Christians have a way to overcome sexual addiction. When a Christian begins the journey to wellness from sexual addiction, they should expect a period of depression. Depression occurs after giving up something that used to come first in their life. Each sexual addiction encounter tapped into the pleasure center of the brain, using plenty of dopamine (the pleasure chemical in the brain). The addict can no longer get the same pleasure from an ordinary sex act. The addict becomes torn, knowing the depression is due to something they thought was pleasurable, but something that had to be stopped or it would destroy them. The addict doesn't necessarily want to stop, but life has become too difficult to continue as is.

Below are key steps to help Christians move forward from sexual addiction.

1. The Christian will need to die daily to themselves and allow Jesus to help them one day at a time.

2. The daily use of negative / positive imaging is recommended. Write down and create several negative images that happened to you while actively involved in your sexual addiction. Practice thinking about these negative images when you see a trigger to act out sexually. Hopefully, the negative image will become an involuntary response that your mind continues to implement daily in your thoughts.

3. Write down positive images that have been created since you've been in recovery. Detail them in your mind and set goals around them so they can be enhanced. Remember—one relapse

will have you starting all over again. All the good that's happened in your recovery will be wiped out. Positive imagery can help you avoid this outcome.

4. Ask God daily to remove the desire for abnormal sex and create a desire to have pleasurable sex with your wife or husband.

5. Read a verse of scripture daily—use that verse as a mantra in your comings and goings for just that day. Chew on it and take it deep inside your mind.

6. Ask several friends or a Christian sponsor who understands what you're going through to accept a phone call from you or meet with you when you're having cues and triggers that can lead to relapse.

7. Avoid people, places, and things that trigger you. You know what those things are and may want to journal them to keep the negative image about them as well.

8. Don't keep secrets, especially regarding temptation. If there's been forgiveness in your marriage, then ask your wife or husband if it's okay to be transparent with them. If it's not okay, then honor their boundaries.

9. Seek a counselor who has experience in sex addiction. Perhaps seek out a Christian counselor who specializes in sex therapy for couples. Your sexual health has been compromised and your marriage's sexual health has been also compromised. The marriage will need to be repaired with respect to sexual pleasure in your relationship.

Finally, the Ultimate Danger Zone for a Believer

The Christian will experience spiritual darkness—not to be confused with depression (psychological darkness), but rather total darkness, with a break in communication with the Lord. For a Christian, this is a dangerous and uncomfortable place, due to the difficulty of getting the fellowship back with the Lord. After sexually acting out, staying in recovery is the way back to peace and light.

As a Christian, the ultimate negative image is the daily darkness that overtakes your life in the wake of your addiction. Say to yourself, "I don't want to grieve the Holy Spirit. I want an intimate and sweet fellowship with my Lord and Savior Jesus Christ." You can look back at the times you were in spiritual darkness, seeing yourself separated from God, with a break in your fellowship with Him. When the desire to relapse comes, slip immediately into the negative image you have created. Daily contrast that with your positive image, to maintain strength against temptations. Take a daily look at the progress you've made by writing in your journal—a result of being in remission from sexual addiction. Remember—the positive things that have happened in your life due to your ongoing recovery would be wiped out with one relapse. A sex addict's daily mantra can be, "My addiction was my bondage, but my recovery is my freedom."

Journaling for Your Daily Soul Food

1. How are you taking care of yourself in these troubling times?

_____

_____

_____

_____

_____

_____

_____

_____

_____

2. List the changes in your life from the beginning until the present as your sexual addiction has progressed.

_____

_____

_____

_____

_____

_____

_____

_____

_____

_____

_____

_____

3. Describe ways you can draw closer to the Lord.

_____

_____

_____

_____

_____

_____

_____

_____

_____

_____

_____

3. Describe ways your family can be a support for you without enabling or shaming.

_____

_____

_____

_____

_____

_____

_____

_____

_____

_____

_____

In closing: the sex addict and their family member need to know there's hope for combating the disease of any addiction. The Christian has the tools within the word of God to defeat the struggle of addiction. The Holy Spirit will be a guide and comfort in the recovery phase. Jesus paid for all your sins and shortcomings. Addiction can go from bondage to freedom.

GODSPEED!